RISE UP

Jesus is the Restorer

Revelations 3:11 (ESV)
I AM coming soon. Hold fast to what you have,
so that no one may seize your crown.

TAMMY J. GLENN

Rise Up

ISBN: 9781097348466
Independently Published

Printed in the United States of America
Edited: Barb Elliot, eBooksByBarb.biz
Layout/Design: Booknook.biz
Cover Design: Shelley Savoy, SM Designs

Dedicated to all the believers who are persecuted daily but continue to be bold for Christ and to those who have lost their lives following Jesus

CONTENTS

ACKNOWLEDGEMENTS

I want to thank the Lord for standing by my side and helping me to write this book. Never in my wildest imagination did I think I could write a book, but here we are on the second book. The Lord has been my friend and shepherd, not only through this process, but in my life for the last 14 years.

I will never quit telling about the day I turned my life over to You, Lord, and if You keep on giving me stories, I will keep on writing them down for others to read. All Glory to Jesus.

Thank you to my husband for being my best friend and always encouraging me to continue to write and for loving me just as I am. You are my Rock.

To my Boog, you are my sunshine! Thank you for always being there for me and encouraging me. I have loved watching you grow as my beautiful daughter, spiritually and as a wife and mother. What a complete blessing you are to my life. You are probably one of the bravest and strongest people I know, and I am so proud of you!

To Sophia, Maddox and Leo, you each bring so much joy to my life! I thank God for each of you every day. Your smiles literally fill the room with light! Each one of you is so special. Don't ever forget that Jesus loves you.

To my brother Patrick who was the writer in our family and is now in Heaven. I know that you are celebrating this victory the Lord has given to me, and if you were here, you would be giving me one of your special hugs that lifted us off our feet. Miss you, Pat!

Thank you to all my prayer partners and all of the people who have prayed with me and for me. I am so thankful to each of you. Know that your prayers have held me up.

Thank you to every person who took the time to email me and send me your very personal testimonies after reading my last book Redeemed. I truly loved that you shared your personal experiences with me it was such a blessing to hear from each of you!

To all my family and friends you mean the world to me: I love you!

INTRODUCTION

2 Corinthians 5:17 (KJV)

*Therefore if any man be in Christ, he is a
new creature: old things are passed away;
behold, all things are become new.*

Jeremiah 30:17 (ESV)

*For I will restore health to you, and your wounds
I will heal, declares the Lord, because
they have called you an outcast:*

We all love to see the Lord bring restoration and healing to the broken and abandoned. It is a beautiful thing to see and experience. This is what the Lord is doing in my own life. These stories are the evidence of God working in my life, as it is by the grace of God that I am able to put them down on paper for others to read and understand that the Lord is always with us.

Jesus is the master storyteller. If you read the Word you will see His stories are full of life, because the Word of God is alive. If we are looking, we will notice that each of our lives is full of these great stories with Jesus in the middle. He is with us in the good, and He is with us in the worst of our days. He never leaves us.

My hope for this book is that it will help you to see that we serve a God who desires each of us to have restoration, and this process will cause you to rise up and be bold for Christ. I said this in my last book and I am saying it again: Your story is important – You are important – You are chosen for this very time in life – Rise up and know that you are royalty in the eyes of our Lord!

RISE UP

*16 "Don't be afraid," the prophet answered.
"Those who are with us are more than
those who are with them."*

*17 And Elisha prayed, "Open his eyes, Lord, so
that he may see." Then the Lord opened
the servant's eyes, and he looked and saw
the hills full of horses and chariots of
fire all around Elisha.*

2 Kings 6:16-17 (NIV)

Lord, open our eyes so that we are able to see that those who are with us are greater than those who are with the enemy.

As I am preparing to write this book, wondering how I am going to start it, the Lord reminds me of a dream I had at the beginning of 2019.

I became aware in my dream that I was in a church. I began walking down a hallway and then entered an auditorium type of room where there was a band playing. As I listened to the music they were playing, it did not seem right in my spirit, so I decided to leave. As I walked outside, it seemed like there were a lot of people outside wandering about, almost like church had just finished.

I started looking for my car but could not find it. I could not remember where I parked. As I looked up at the sky, the clouds darkened and started turning into angels that came flying down on the earth. When they hit the ground, they turned into bears. It seemed like they ran through the people, not physically knocking them down but spiritually right through them.. Then I looked up again and I saw the sky full of angels in color.

When I looked around me, I noticed that some people were moving about as if they saw nothing, and others like myself saw what I saw. I was terrified at first, but then I became very calm at the second look.

I was trying to go home but could not find anyone that I had gone to church with and still could not find my own car. I then found myself at the front of the church calling a taxi. As the phone began to ring I woke up. As I began to ask the Lord about my dream, all I really got was that the Lord would show me its meaning, which I feel He has revealed to me as I began writing this book.

I came out of the church because I did not like the music that was being played. I was offended by the music.

Matthew 24:10 (NKJV)
10 And then many will be offended

As I looked up and the clouds darkened and turned into angels and then into bears as they touched down on the earth –

Ephesians 6:12 (NKJV)
¹² For we do not wrestle against flesh and blood, but
against principalities, against powers, against the rulers
of the darkness of this age, against spiritual hosts of
wickedness in the heavenly places.

We are in a spiritual battle right now. Some people see it and some do not. Deception and blinders are up because many are offended.

My second glance was filled with peace because the Lord removed my blinders to show me that those that are with us are far greater than those with the enemy.

2 Kings 6:16
¹⁶ "Don't be afraid," the prophet answered. "Those who
are with us are more than those who are with them."

I went back to the front of the church because a sheep that has been separated from the flock will never make it.

Ecclesiastes 4:12 (NLT)
A person standing alone can be
attacked and defeated, but two can stand
back-to-back and conquer. Three are even better,
for a triple-braided cord is not easily broken.

The Lord says in Acts 2:17 (NIV) and Joel 2:28 (NIV),

'In the last days, God says, I will pour out my Spirit on all people. Your sons and daughters will prophesy, your young men will see visions, your old men will dream dreams.

The Lord will use dreams and visions to speak to us and I believe that this is a clear message. We are in a battle, and it is not visible to the human eye unless you have spiritual eyes.

The Lord is warning us that offense is going to be everywhere and that when we become offended (offended people are hateful, angry, bitter, resentful, unforgiving, jealous, hurtful, and the list goes on), we open the door for blinders and deception to have a place in our lives (and in our hearts), to entangle us and lead us astray, away from God.

We are not to walk in fear because there are far more with and for us than could ever be against us. Walk by faith, trusting in Jesus. Do not allow yourself to become isolated, because when we are separated from other believers we are easy prey and more likely to listen to the lies of our enemy. He is a liar and a thief who wants to kill and destroy us. We have been chosen for this very time, and I feel as though the Lord is calling us to rise up and be not afraid. Below are the scriptures that the Lord gave me to confirm this dream.

What the bear represents

Revelation 13:2 (KJV)
Illustrative of the kingdom of Anti-Christ:
² And the beast which I saw was like unto a leopard, and his feet were as the feet of a bear, and his mouth as the mouth of a lion: and the dragon gave him his power, and his seat, and great authority.

Daniel 7:5 (NASB)
Illustrative of the kingdom of the Medes:
And behold, another beast, a second one, resembling a bear. And it was raised up on one side, and three ribs were in its mouth between its teeth; and thus they said to it, 'Arise, devour much meat!'

Proverbs 28:15 (NAS 1977)
Illustrative of wicked rulers:
Like a roaring lion and a rushing bear Is a wicked ruler over a poor people.

1 Samuel 17:34 (NASB)
Attacks the flock in the presence of the shepherd:
But David said to Saul, "Your servant was tending his father's sheep. When a lion or a bear came and took a lamb from the flock,

2 Kings 2:24 (NASB)
Often attacks man:
When he looked behind him and saw them, he cursed
them in the name of the LORD. Then two female bears
came out of the woods and tore up
forty-two lads of their number.

Prayer:

Lord, help us to stay close to You. Fill us with humility, love, boldness, wisdom, understanding, and discernment. We pray for forgiveness for any offenses against You or anyone else we may be offended by. Close any doors we may have opened and fill us with Your peace that surpasses understanding. We ask You to remove the blinders from us and help us to see the truth. Expose any and all deception in our lives. May we stay united with other believers, holding the ground You have given us. May we be warriors for the Kingdom of Heaven.

In Jesus' name.

Amen

'MAKE STRAIGHT THE WAY FOR THE LORD.'

Isaiah 40:3 (NIV)

A voice of one calling: "In the wilderness prepare the way for the LORD; make straight in the desert a highway for our God. ..."

John 1:23 (NIV)

John replied in the words of Isaiah the prophet, "I am the voice of one calling in the wilderness, 'Make straight the way for the Lord.'"

As I sat in my prayer chair this morning, I wondered to myself, *can one person really make a difference?* And these words are what I heard in my spirit:

"I heard a voice crying in the wilderness."

The Lord gave me Isaiah 40:3 and John 1:23. John the Baptist went into the wilderness to prepare the way for the coming of our Lord Jesus. I wonder if, as he sat by himself, he may have thought the very words I myself thought this morning: *Can one person make a difference? Am I doing this right, Lord? Did I hear you right, Lord?*

Do you ever feel like you are in the wilderness wondering if anyone will hear you? Do you think John could have imagined that he would be the one to baptize the Son of God, our Lord and savior Jesus The Christ?

God called John to proclaim that Jesus was coming and tell the people they should open their hearts, repent, and get ready to see because the Messiah was coming! One day John was in the wilderness alone; the next day he was baptizing the Lord Jesus. He literally saw the Holy Spirit descending upon Jesus. He saw the heavens open up and heard the audible voice of God!

I am hearing this voice calling right now to each of us, saying, "Get ready, be prepared, be looking for Me. Lean not on your own understanding. The Lord is coming soon." (Luke 21:25-28 KJV)

No matter how the devil attacks you with thoughts of insecurity, unworthiness, wanting to quit, or maybe, like the thought that came to me this morning, doubt: "Can one person really make a difference?" And yes, that was a thought from the enemy. He is always trying to move us out of the will of God, and that always starts with a thought. Can one person really make a difference? Are you sure you heard God? Will it really matter if you write this story down? If you do not take the thought captive immediately, you will be meditating on something that is not the will of God.

We need to press on, knowing full well that our voice in the body is so very important and that we will make a difference.

Your voice, when speaking the Truth, is the light that goes forward, pushing darkness down until it exists no more. The same as John's voice went forward and people came from all over to hear him preach the Word of God. Although I am sure darkness tried to prevent John from speaking the truth, we know the truth won that battle. The light (the Word of God) went forward and drew people to itself.

There is a voice crying out, and it is the Holy Spirit crying to each of us to be the voice of truth and walk in love, the kind of love that tells the truth regardless of how popular it is. The Word of God is called the good news for a reason: because it is good news that brings redemption, freedom, healing, and Love.

'Make straight the way for the Lord.'"

Rise up, stand firm, hold your ground, and walk in the victory the Lord has already given to you

Dear Lord,

Help us to remember that You have called each of us and have a purpose for each of our lives. May the words of our mouths be anointed by the Holy Spirit. Help us to speak lovingly yet boldly, so that our words might pierce the hearts of the people. We pray that we speak words of wisdom and truth that do not go out void or return void. Soften our hearts and equip us to be warriors for the Kingdom of Heaven.

'Make straight the way for the Lord.'

In Jesus' name, amen.

Ezra 10:4 (ESV)
Arise, for it is your task, and we are with you; be strong and do it.

BE BOLD

Boldness, which means "freedom from timidity" or "liberty" according to Webster's 1828 dictionary, is a basic character trait every Christian needs to have.

Proverbs 28:1 (NIV)

The wicked flee though no one pursues, but the righteous are as bold as a lion.

Acts 4:31 (NIV)

[31] After they prayed, the place where they were meeting was shaken. And they were all filled with the Holy Spirit and spoke the word of God boldly.

When you are following Jesus the stories just pile up, and if we don't write them down, they will simply slip away. I hate to say this, but I had quit writing for some time after my last book, *Redeemed*. It was a literal war writing that book, and honestly, when I was done writing it, I thought that it was a one-time assignment from the Lord. But I started to feel the Holy Spirit nudging me to write again. And when I was called out for a job, these people sparked my heart and gave me a desire to write down this story.

Working as a mobile notary I get to meet all kinds of people. On this particular day I was called for an assignment, and the company who contracted me actually warned me that the woman, Rose (name has been changed), who needed to sign the documents that I was taking to her, had severe anxiety.

When I arrived at the location, the first thing I noticed was that it was in a rough area. I pulled into the parking spot, and as I looked up, I saw a young boy peering out of one of the upstairs windows that looked as if they had sheets hanging from them. All I could think was "Lord Jesus, please protect me." I always pray before every assignment, but I was still very nervous going in.

The young boy answered the door with an unlit cigarette in his hand. As I walked through the door, his mom Rose was standing with her back to me at the kitchen sink. She did not turn around immediately to greet me but kept her back to me. I said hello to her and then explained I had the documents for her case to sign. I then asked if this was a good time to sign them. She turned to me, replied, "Yes," and seemed very nice. We went into the living room to sit.

As I started to get out the documents, she began to tell me about her son James (name has been changed). He had some medical issues from complications at birth. She began to confess her anxiety and depression to me — which I can tell you is a very common thing that happens because I am asking the Lord to use me, and although I am a stranger, people will confess things without knowing why. This is what opens the door to talk about Jesus and allows me to know how to pray for them.

I then asked if she believed in Jesus, to which she replied "Yes," that she used to go to church with her grandmother until the grandmother passed on, but that she had not been to church since then. I told her how God delivered me from alcohol and drugs and that if He did it for me, He would do the same for her.

As James sat and listened, I told them about a local church, and James said, "Yes! I want to go to church." He told me that the church I was talking about had come to his school!

There was something special about James. He also had a story, and he started to tell me how he had been bullied at school. As I sat and listened to him, I became very aware that although he had been bullied, he still had so much love in his heart.

I explained to him that only someone who was hurting themselves could bully another person because anyone who was filled with joy would not want to harm someone else. I wanted him to remember and know that it was not him that had the problem, but the problem was within the other child.

I began to share my own personal testimony, and their reaction to my testimony was so joyous that it touched my heart deeply. Once again the Lord was showing me how important it is to share with others the things we have been set free from and how much God loves us. I told Rose that when I wrote my testimony, I asked the Lord, "Who is going to want to read this?"

As soon as I said it, she held my book to her heart and said, "Me! Me!" I wanted to cry at that moment because I too often believe the voice of the enemy, who continually tells me I am unimportant and unqualified. We finished up the signing, and I told them they would love the local church and that I would be praying for them.

As I walked out, James followed me to my car and stood outside my window smiling at me. My heart felt such joy.

While pulling out of the parking lot I realized once again how, when we go out into the world hoping to make an impact for the Kingdom, the Lord can turn that and use it to impact our own lives. Although they were hurting, they had not hardened their hearts; they were open to hearing and receiving the Lord.

I let Jesus come with me into that house, and He used me and my testimony to lift this family up. There was a time after the Lord started healing me when I just wanted to forget those things behind me. I did not want to be in vulnerable positions or show my emotions because I thought that was weak and I was ashamed of things I had done. Now I know that it is in our weakness that He is made strong. He uses all our brokenness to touch others and show them they too can have restoration.

Be Bold for Christ -

Lord, help each of us to be bold, for the time is short and there are so many hurting people who need to hear our testimonies. Help us to encourage others to be bold for Christ. I pray that you help us go out with soft hearts and listening ears, filled with the Holy Spirit.

In Jesus' name. Amen.

Acts 26:16 (NIV)
Now get up and stand on your feet. I have appeared to you to appoint you as a servant and as a witness of what you have seen and will see of me.

YOU WILL DO GREATER THINGS

John 14:12 (NIV)

I tell you the truth, anyone who has faith in me will do what I have been doing. He will do even greater things than these, because I am going to the Father.

"The greater things" the Lord is referring to here is talking about when Jesus returns to the Father and sends His Holy Spirit to dwell in each of us, we will multiply in number. As we increase, so do the miracles, because the power and love of God have increased.

It is said in John 21:25 that all the books in the whole world cannot contain the miracles that Jesus Himself did. Can you imagine how many miraculous stories there are now by the power of the Holy Spirit dwelling in each of us!

I know that many of you reading this have maybe lost someone very significant to you. I lost my mom a little over two years ago, and there are still days it seems hard to believe she is gone. As I headed out for a walk recently, I was feeling emotional thinking about her. Some days it is so raw, and then other days I have peace because I know she is with Jesus. As I turned the corner and headed to my dog's favorite tree, I slowed and heard in my spirit, "You will do greater things," to which I replied in my spirit that "I cannot do this without you, Lord." I felt tears well up inside of me as I said this, and at that moment I looked down at the ground and saw a penny lying right next to my foot.

I read a book years ago called *The Penny* by Joyce Meyer. In the book, the penny she found was an answer to prayer, and she discovered it was God's way of telling her He loved her. Oftentimes when I have needed to know God is there or that He loves me, I would see a penny. When I picked up the penny, for some reason I thought it was going to be a 1967, the year I was born. I have no idea why I thought that, but it was not. It was the year 2016, the year my mom passed. This is what my cousin calls a "God wink." Why do you think the Lord used this particular time to tell me "You are going to do greater things"?

It's at a time when I feel weak that He decides *yes, it's a good time to tell her she is going to do great things.* Because it is at these times when we are most attentive to His voice. We stop, we listen, we hear, and we know at that very moment we have heard the small, still voice of the Lord.

I also know that when the Lord starts to lead us in a new direction or starts to plant a desire to do something for the Kingdom (as He was preparing me to write this book), the devil likes to lead us away from that mission. The Lord wanted me to see that penny because that is what Love does: it lifts us up. He wanted me to know *yes, 2016 was the year your mom passed, and I love her too.* When we hurt, so does Jesus.

When the Lord starts to move in our lives, the devil always wants to drag us back to the past. I have been attacked by a spirit of grief so great that I was unsure I would make it through. The Lord does not want me going back and allowing the thoughts of the enemy to try to steal what He is doing in my life right now. I love how God snatched up that moment of hurt and pain and filled it with His love – something only He can do.

We are entering a time when we are going to see the greatest miracles ever. We are going to see a move of God like we have never seen before. God has a message: He is going to do great things in our lives, and each of us is going to do great things for the Kingdom. Listen for the voice of God and don't be afraid to do whatever He has put in your heart.

You are going to do greater things!

Father,

We come to You in the name of Jesus. By the Blood of Christ, help us to do Your will. Let us not be distracted by our enemy; help us to stay focused on Your plan for us. When we go out into the world, we ask that You will open and close the doors that You have chosen for us. Thank You, Lord, for we are going to do great things for the Kingdom, and we give You all the glory.

In Jesus' name, Amen.

Isaiah 52:2 (ESV)
Shake yourself from the dust and arise;

ARISE LIKE A LIONESS

Numbers 23:24 (NIV)

The people rise like a lioness; they rouse themselves like a lion that does not rest till it devours its prey and drinks the blood of its victims.

Luke 4:18-19 (NIV)

"The Spirit of the Lord is on me, because he has anointed me to proclaim good news to the poor. He has sent me to proclaim freedom for the prisoners and recovery of sight for the blind, to set the oppressed free, to proclaim the year of the Lord's favor."

On February 12, 2019, I woke up and sat in my prayer chair to hear these words: "Arise like a lioness." As I meditated on the word "lioness," the Lord gave me Numbers 23:24. I sensed in my spirit that we are being called to come out of our safe places, wake up, step out of our comfort zones, and pray for ears to hear what the Holy Spirit is saying to each of us.

One of the greatest lies from our enemy is that we need to wait until we are made perfect, with no flaws, to do the Lord's work. We will never achieve this until we have arrived in Heaven. There is never going to be a day when we will feel ready to do the Lord's work because Satan works against us at all times. Even as I write this,

I am plagued with thoughts of things I need to do or should do, or my phone is dinging. I then have to turn to the Lord and say, "Make these words your weapon, Lord. Raise up the army You want to go forth. Give us the boldness, courage, wisdom, understanding, and discernment to do Your will and Your work. Raise up the watchmen, the prayer warriors, the healers, the praise teams, the deliverers, the evangelists, the pastors, the teachers, the writers, and the workers, and fill them with Your Spirit in Jesus' name!"

About two days after the Lord gave me "arise like a lioness," I was cleaning my room and found a book my husband had given to me called *Lioness Arising: Wake Up and Change Your World* by Lisa Bevere. I turned the book over and the very scripture the Lord led me to – Numbers 23:24 – was on the back of this book.

Now, my husband had given this book to me in 2017 along with two of her other books, but for some reason this one I had pushed aside and had not read. The Word the Lord gave me at the beginning of this year, 2019, was "Rise up."

Of course, I snatched this book up and read it immediately.

While reading this book, I found a few things that really stood out to me that fell right in line with what I felt the Lord was saying to me.

Micah 4:13 (MSG)
On your feet, Daughter of Zion! Be threshed of chaff,
be refined of dross. I'm remaking you into a people
invincible...

Wake up – Rise up – Know who you are in Christ – Be the light of Christ –

Be up and awake to what God is doing –

You are Royalty in the eyes of Jesus –

Without knowing who you are in Christ you will lose vision and purpose

God will use a storm to awaken you just like He did with
Jonah, Do not run like Jonah – Jonah 4:1-2

God did not save you to tame you –

The word "Christian" means "anointed" or "Christlike one." Everything Jesus did had action behind it –

This is going to look different for every person reading this. The Lord has placed inside of each of us something different. He has placed inside of me the strongest desire to save souls. I have a desire to see people delivered from the bondages that have held them down. I know this can happen because the Lord delivered me from alcohol and drugs.

As I talk to my daughter Brooke about rising up, she tells me she too is hearing in her spirit, "Rise up." She says that she is drawn to speak out for people who are weak, in need, such as sexual assault victims, children, and the broken.

What is the Lord saying to you? Just take one step and watch the doors open for you. In this process you will discover the Lord healing you and loving you deeper and deeper in places you did not even know existed.

Stepping out in faith oftentimes starts small, such as helping a neighbor, taking care of an elderly parent, teaching your children about the Lord, buying a meal for someone, volunteering at a shelter or your church, going to Bible study, driving someone to an appointment, and so on. These small acts of love open the door for the Lord to do greater things and that is how it happens: One door after another opens, and you are moving in the Body of Christ. That voice that said, "Can one person really make a difference?" is now being silenced.

When reading about lionesses I learned that they are completely devoted to the lion. The lioness is a fierce protector of her cubs and also the provider of food for the lion, while the lion protects the lioness at all times. They work hand in hand with each other, much like a husband and wife. Each of us is the bride of Christ, as it says in the Word that Jesus is the Bridegroom. He is the

Lion. Jesus goes before us, and we should understand that He is coming back for His bride.

Revelation 5:5 (NIV) says:
Then one of the elders said to me, "Do not weep! See,
the Lion of the tribe of Judah, the Root of David,
has triumphed. He is able to open the scroll and its
seven seals."

Jesus is the Lion and we each are His lioness, we are His bride. He will protect us at all costs, even at the great cost of giving up His life for us. But we are not to weep, because He has now become the King of all kings and the Lord of all lords and has triumphed over our enemy!!

Lord, help us to arise from our slumber and we ask You to arise, O Lord.

We thank You that Your enemies will be scattered as we go out to do Your will. It is not by our power or our might but by Your Spirit that we will have the victory.

In Jesus' name we pray. Amen.

I AM with you, says the Lord (Isaiah 41:10 NIV)

Numbers 10:35 (NIV)
Whenever the ark set out, Moses said, "Rise up,
LORD! May your enemies be scattered; may your
foes flee before you."

RAW AND REAL

John 1:5 (NIV)

The light shines in darkness, and darkness has not overcome it.

2 Corinthians 4:2 (NASB)

but we have renounced the things hidden because of shame, not walking in craftiness or adulterating the word of God, but by the manifestation of truth commending ourselves to every man's conscience in the sight of God.

When I went to write my first book *Redeemed,* I wrote and rewrote those pages so many times. Wanting to give up, I sought out the Lord and I felt as though He spoke to me and said, "Be raw and real. Do not add to the stories and do not take away from the stories." Because it is in our vulnerability that people relate. We want to hide the ugly stuff and just tell about the good, but that is not real life.

One of the things the Lord does after you have turned your life over to Him is shine a light into the dark places inside of you. You see, shame likes to hide way down deep, and until something comes into the light, it will stay hidden, and if it's hidden, then it has power.

So in my first book I briefly mentioned that I had an abortion at a very young age. I want you to know that I put that in the book and took it out of the book so many times. You see, I did not want to tell my daughter about it. I was so filled with shame and self-hate that I just simply wanted it to go away. But I discovered something after I told her. She did not hate me, she forgave me, and shame was broken off of me.

I hate that I made that decision, but the fact is I cannot go back and change that decision. The only way to heal is to bring it into the light and allow the Lord to work. Because of this deep root of shame and guilt, it silenced me. Even the few people that knew did not know what I was feeling inside, they just knew that I had done it. All those thoughts of self-hate went inward where the voice of our enemy used it against me.

Even right now I would never had chosen this topic to put in this book, but this is what the Lord is leading me to write about. Recently I responded to a post on social media telling a part of my story about having an abortion. Truly, I expected backlash, but what happened was the opposite. The outpouring of love I received from other broken and silenced women made me cry. When I started to read the stories of other women who also had abortions, and the shame and pain they also had faced, I started to see how the enemy works both sides of this. The enemy makes you think it is the solution, and then afterwards you are covered in guilt and shame or you just harden your heart, burying it deep within, hoping to forget it.

I am telling you this story because there may be something in your life, like there was in mine, that wants to hold you hostage from the Lord and keep you from doing the Lord's work. Shame is a prison that holds us hostage.

There is no unforgiveable sin. We like to lay sins out in a particular order, from what we think are the worst to the least bad. That is not how the Kingdom of God works. That is why Jesus points out in Matthew 5:28 NIV that even if you look at another with lust, you have committed adultery. He wanted to make sure all those who think their sin is not as bad as their friend or neighbor's that actually it is. No one is getting into Heaven without the precious Blood of Jesus covering them, and there is no sin that is more powerful than the Blood of Jesus.

The enemy will use these things to hold us back from rising up in the Kingdom of God. He will use anything he can to stop you from fulfilling your purpose that the Lord has for you. Satan is not so concerned with your salvation as much as he is with stealing your purpose and your voice for the Kingdom of God.

I carried this around for 32 years locked up. We serve a God of forgiveness, and when He died on that cross He paid a high price for you and me. I want you to know that although I was scared to reveal something I did that was not right, I am so glad that I did, because it no longer has any power over me. I am free from the condemnation of our enemy and also of myself. We are commanded to forgive others, and this includes forgiving oneself also. And at times it has been harder for me to forgive myself than others. Being real and honest will set you free, and you will rise up and walk in the freedom that Jesus wants you to have.

Thank You, Lord, for Your supernatural healing power. Thank You that shame is bound off of each of us by Your precious Blood. We pray for healing in the deepest parts of our hearts. Help us to be honest with You, Lord, so that we can be free from the hurts of our past. Thank you, Father, that You tell us in Your Word we are forgiven as far as the east is to the west. Help us to be the overcomers You have created us to be. Who the Son sets free is free indeed.

In Jesus' name, Amen.

Romans 8:1 (KJV)
There is therefore now no condemnation to them which are in Christ Jesus, who walk not after the flesh, but after the Spirit.

Luke 5:23-24 (KJV)
Whether is easier, to say, Thy sins be forgiven thee; or to say, Rise up and walk? But that ye may know that the Son of man hath power upon earth to forgive sins, (he said unto the sick of the palsy,) I say unto thee, Arise, and take up thy couch, and go into thine house.

STAND FIRM

Psalms 94:16 (KJV)

Who will rise up for me against the evildoers? Or who will stand up for me against the workers of iniquity?

I watched a movie recently called *I'm Not Ashamed*. It is the true story of a young girl named Rachel (played by Masey McLain) and her life as a believer in Christ at Columbine High School before the shooting which occurred in 1999. This day is still in my memory, and I was struck with how quickly time had gone by; it has been 20 years. It then reminded me of the scripture James 4:14 (NIV): "Why, you do not even know what will happen tomorrow. What is your life? You are a mist that appears for a little while and then vanishes."

I also saw a sermon preached by Francis Chan about this very topic. In the sermon he held up a rope about 50 feet long and showed the portion on the rope that represented our life on Earth, which was about one inch in length. The rest of the approximately 50-foot rope represented our time in eternity. I imagine Rachel going to school that day in 1999. She probably never thought, *This could be my last day here on Earth.*

Time is precious, and what we do with our time matters, right now and also when we enter Heaven. The Word says we will not be judged for our sins because Jesus has paid the penalty for those sins, but we are rewarded for the things we have done for the Kingdom of Heaven while we are here on Earth. (1 Corinthians 3:12-14 ESV, Revelation 20:12-13 ESV, Matthew10:41-42)

In the life of this young girl, this movie shows how she struggles in her walk with Jesus – the world is pulling her in one direction and her love for Christ pulls her back – she is tormented because she has not fully committed to Jesus, but there comes a moment in her life that she has to rise up for Christ. All the lies of the world unfold around her, and she understands that the love we try to get from the world is circumstantial love, a changing love, a conditional love, and a love that can be very deceiving. The blinders come off, and she understands that the love of Christ is unconditional, forgiving, and an unchanging love that can never be moved, no matter what we have done or said. She stands up in a class of her peers and proclaims her faith in Jesus Christ. The class is uncomfortable, they shift in their seats.

This can be the same way in our own lives. People shifted in their seats when I gave my life to Jesus. Some came around me, some fled, some stood at a distance and just watched, and some people rejoiced just as the angels in Heaven do. As the Word says, when one sinner repents, there is a literal party in Heaven! (Luke 15:10 NIV)

That day that Rachel stood up in class there was a party in heaven. We are all going to face these moments where we are going to want to fit in with the world, but the fact is we do not belong to this world (John 15:18-19). Although people made fun of her and mocked her, Rachel stood firm in her faith in Christ because, when you know the truth, you will not bend or waver for a lie.

If you have already given your life to Jesus and you are living to please the world, the Lord is calling you right now to come back. The Lord loves you, and we as the Body of Christ need you. You are a warrior for the Kingdom of God. He chose you for this very time in life and is calling you to come back.

If you have never given your life to Jesus, then this is a call to invite you into the Kingdom of Heaven. Romans 10:9 says that if you confess with your mouth that "Jesus is Lord" and believe in your heart that God raised Him from the dead, you will be saved. I heard a pastor say one time that the Book of John was written so that a man might believe, so I think that is always a good place to start to read.

Although Rachel lost her life that horrible day in 1999, she gained her life in eternity, and because she stood firm in her faith for Jesus and because she stood her ground, many souls were saved and continue to be saved. The Lord took her beautiful testimony and made this movie that millions have now seen. I wonder how many have given their lives to Jesus because Rachel stood firm.

Be not ashamed of Christ. Rise up and be the child of God He created you to be!

Lord, thank You for the testimony Rachel shared with this world. I pray that, in a similar situation, fear would not overtake us, and that we too would have the courage to share our own testimonies. Forgive us for allowing the enemy to use shame and fear to hold us back from proclaiming the Glory of Your Kingdom. Let us stand firm in Your love that surrounds us and be the child of God You have created each of us to be. May Your purpose be fulfilled in our lives in and on this earth as it is in Heaven. Your will, Lord, not ours.

In Jesus' name we pray. Amen.

Isaiah 57:1 (NIV)
The righteous perish, and no one takes it to heart; the devout are taken away, and no one understands that the righteous are taken away to be spared from evil.

CHOOSE FREEDOM

John 15:15 (NIV)

I no longer call you servants, because a servant does not know his master's business. Instead, I have called you friends, for everything that I learned from my Father I have made known to you.

Galatians 5:1 (ESV)

"For freedom Christ has set us free; stand firm therefore, and do not submit again to a yoke of slavery."

I love the scripture John 15:15 because it is teaching us that Jesus is one with the Father, and that when we choose to serve the Lord, we are not serving Him as a slave, one who is forced. No… He is saying we are friends, and that by walking with Jesus, we will have knowledge about who our Father is and how much He loves us. Then the second scripture, Galatians 5:1, is saying that by the precious Blood of Jesus, we have been freed from the yoke of slavery, and then it says, "So don't go back."

There are two masters wooing us to serve them: we have Jesus and Satan. Jesus is wooing us to come into the light to be set free, and at the same time, your enemy is wooing you to come back into slavery. When we break free by the power of God from alcohol, drugs, pornography, food, gossip, hate, anger, bitterness, resentment, jealousy, and so on, we have a choice: will we stand firm in our freedom that Jesus paid for us to have or will we go back to our old master and serve him? Every choice we make opens doors unto good or evil. Standing firm and holding the ground that God gives us is the freedom Christ bought for us.

The Lord delivered me from a 27-year addiction to alcohol. He removed the desire to drink so it was as if I had never drunk a day in my life. I do not think about it, nor do I desire to drink. But I had to make a very clear choice: was I going to drink or not drink? It was a matter of standing firm in my decision. I let my "no" be "no." In James 5:12 it says, "Let your yes be yes and your no be no or you will be condemned." In other words, we cannot be double-minded.

I like to think back to that day when the ownership of my life changed hands. As the pastor made the altar call and I got up and started for the front of that church, the old master was screaming for me to come back: "You don't belong here, they will never accept you, you are unworthy, God will never love you." At the same time this was happening, warrior angels came forward: "Go forward. 'You are mine,' says the Lord. You are loved." I imagine the angels were bubbling inside, getting ready to sing and rejoice, the war was so real.

Inside I was filled with complete fear, but I kept walking to the front of that church, where I got down on my knees and declared Jesus was my Lord. The chains fell away, the door opened, and Satan became powerless. He no longer had any ownership over me or my life. When I stood up, the congregation had come forward, surrounding me, and as they started hugging me, this love completely surrounded me.

The thing about slavery/bondage is that you have to renew your mind. You are no longer a slave, but if you continue to listen to the lies of the old master, you will never be free. You don't have to be in prison to be a prisoner. As a matter of fact, there are people who are in prison that have received Jesus as their savior who are living in more freedom than people living in the world who do not have Jesus.

Meditate on what the Lord says about you: The Lord says you are loved, you have the mind of Christ, you are alive in Christ. you are God's workmanship. You are a new creature in Christ. You are chosen. You are royalty. There is no condemnation in Christ. You are a joint-heir with Christ. You are raised up with Christ, and you have been redeemed from the curses of sin, sickness, poverty, spiritual death, and the law. (Romans 1:7, Philippians 2:5, Ephesians 2:5, Ephesians 2:10, 2 Corinthians 5:17, 1 Peter 2:9, Romans 8:1, Romans 8:17, Ephesians 2:6)

If you have given your life to Jesus and are still being held captive, speak out against your enemy with the Word of God. If you are speaking out against your enemy and you are still being attacked, please go and find a believer to pray with you. Remember the Word says to go to the church (read Ephesians).

James 5:14

Is anyone among you sick? Let them call the elders of the church to pray over them and anoint them with oil in the name of the Lord.

Choose Freedom

Dear Lord,
We thank You that the Word of God is alive and sharper than a double-edged sword. Help us to walk in the freedom You desire for each of us to have. Help us to hold the ground You give to us. We ask for Your love to become our weapon when fear and lies come against us as we know these are the tactics the enemy uses to hold us back and they have no power. Help us to rise up out of slavery/bondage.

Do not believe the lies. You are free to choose. Choose Life. Choose the good Master, our Lord Jesus, who came to set the captives free (Luke 4:18)!

2 Corinthians 3:17
Now the Lord is Spirit, and where the Spirit of the Lord
is, there is freedom.

LUKE 16:13 (NIV)

"No one can serve two masters. *Either you will hate the one and love the other, or you will be devoted to the one and despise the other. You cannot serve both God and money."*

SOPHIA'S STORY

Matthew 18:1-5 (KJV)

At the same time came the disciples unto Jesus, saying, Who is the greatest in the kingdom of heaven?

And Jesus called a little child unto him, and set him in the midst of them, And said, Verily I say unto you, Except ye be converted, and become as little children, ye shall not enter into the kingdom of heaven. Whosoever therefore shall humble himself as this little child, the same is greatest in the kingdom of heaven. And whoso shall receive one such little child in my name receiveth me.

I love this scripture because it is so simple. Children are humble and so very honest. They also have the ability to believe without seeing. This is called "faith." Faith is the substance of things hoped for, the evidence of things not seen (Hebrews 11:1).

Sophia has the special ability, as many children do, to simply believe that Jesus is real, and she knows in her heart that He loves her and will always protect her. She says it all the time. When my mom passed on, Sophia was two and half years old. That is pretty young to really understand about Heaven and Jesus, yet Sophia seemed to have no problem understanding it. At random times she would tell me that her great-grandma Judy was with Jesus. We would be driving down the road and she would ask me if I knew that Great-grandma Judy was in the sky with Jesus.

Sophia started pre-school this year and loves it. She usually has all kinds of stories to tell, but on this particular day she really was not telling me a story, she was just simply telling me about the conversation she had with her teacher. She began by telling me that she was talking to her teacher and telling her about Jesus. I then asked her what she said to her teacher and she said, "I told her that did she know that Jesus was alive?" Then Sophia said, "Well, I told her that actually Jesus died, but He came back to life and that now He is alive and lives in Heaven." Then I asked her what her teacher said, and she said her teacher said, "Yes, He is, Sophia." I have no idea what the teacher really thought, but what I understood was how the Lord can and will use the voice of a child to reach out to touch others, and how a child's voice can soften even the hardest of hearts.

The Lord uses the willing, and children are so willing because they believe, and their hearts are so soft and full of love. Who will be offended at a child sharing the gospel? The scripture says: "Whosoever therefore shall humble himself as this little child, the same is greatest in the kingdom of heaven. And whoso shall receive one such little child in my name receiveth me."

So when Sophia's teacher received Sophia's humility, she actually was receiving Jesus that day. The Lord is looking for those who will humble themselves. Oh, how the doors open when we have turned from pride and started walking with humility.

Sophia not only knows that Jesus loves her and will protect her, she knows He is her healer. Just recently she showed me how she fell down and ripped her pants. As she pulled the pant leg back to show me the scrape on her knee, she said, "It's ok, Grandma, because Jesus will heal it." Not more than one hour later she pulled it back again and said, "Look, Grandma, Jesus is healing it!" Then her almost-three-year-old brother Maddox agreed with her and said, "Yes, Jesus is healing it, Grandma!"

My heart grew two sizes just listening to them talk, and actually it made me look inward, desiring to walk in this simple faith like a child. This is the kind of faith the Lord desires for us to walk in. The Lord says to us, "My yoke is easy and my burden is light." (Matthew 11:30 NIV) He tells us, "Don't be afraid; just believe" (Mark 5:36 NIV).

Father, protect our little ones and help us to have faith like a child simply believing that You are who You say You are, that You will take care of us, that You do love us, that we are Yours, that You chose each of us and have a purpose for each of our lives. Help us to rise up with humility and love of the kind Sophia and Maddox have shown to us.

In Jesus' name. Amen.

Isaiah 60:1 (NLV)
"Rise up and shine, for your light has come. The shining-greatness of the Lord has risen upon you."

Matthew 28:6 (NASB)
"He is not here, for He has risen, just as He said. Come, see the place where He was lying."

THE HORSE IS MADE READY

Revelation 19:11,14-16 (NIV)

"¹¹I saw heaven standing open and there before me was a white horse, whose rider is called Faithful and True. ... ¹⁴ The armies of heaven were following him, riding on white horses and dressed in fine linen, white and clean. ¹⁵ Coming out of his mouth is a sharp sword with which to strike down the nations. "He will rule them with an iron scepter." He treads the winepress of the fury of the wrath of God Almighty. ¹⁶ On his robe and on his thigh he has this name written:

King of kings and Lord of lords.

Recently I became a little obsessed with a show called *Heartland*. Maybe not so much the show as I really became more interested in the horses. I started to see how beautiful and intelligent God created this animal. What really struck me was how they can play an intricate part in healing the hearts and souls of broken people. When my uncle had first told me about this show, I had very little interest because I do not watch TV very often. But I had recently loaded Pureflix on my TV, and as I was looking through the shows I came across *Heartland*. This show was on its 11th season – ok, that is 11 years of shows that I was behind. Never did I ever think I would watch all these seasons, but I did. In the very first episode the young star loses her mom, and it starts from this point on a real and raw message about healing, love, family, and life. As I watched this show unfold, it started to touch parts of my heart that I had pushed down.

What I found interesting on this show is that the horse would arrive broken, with certain issues. But the issue was not always with the horse; often it was with the person/owner who then was transferring it to the horse. They would at times bring the person back to find out what issues they were facing, such as anger/anxiety/stress/loss and so on. Once the person let go of what was ailing them, the horse fell in line. Now I'm not a horse expert, but from what I have read, this really does happen. Horses will reflect what you are feeling.

We all have or had brokenness in our hearts, and I have learned over the years that the Lord will use all kinds of things or people to touch that brokenness. I have always been the type of person to bury it and just try to move on, and that is not how healing happens – healing can be ugly and messy. In this busy world we all live in, there seems to be no time for that, but if we are leaning on God and trusting in Him, He will want to restore and heal us in the deepest parts.

So as I mentioned in an earlier story, I do mobile notary work. I accepted a job, and the day I was to go out on this assignment I found myself wanting to cancel. It was a late-night signing that was quite a distance away, and it was going to involve driving back roads in the dark. I really don't like driving back roads, not even in the daylight hours. I decided to go because I had made a commitment and I am so glad I did now, but at the time I was not. Satan always uses fear to try to steer us in another direction. Always.

I arrived safely at the destination and greeted the couple that were to sign the documents I had with me.

I sat down at the table and started to get all the paperwork out. As I was looking around the clients' house, I noticed a picture they had hanging close to where we were sitting. I made a comment about it being so beautiful, for which they thanked me. They then told me that their son, who was still in high school, had drawn the picture. I was so amazed at this young man's talent.

They then told me that he has other pictures that he is selling on Etsy. Would I like to look at them? "Yes," I replied, "I would love to look at them!" We went on to complete our signing, and then their son went downstairs and got his pictures and brought them up for me to look at.

As I look through his pictures, I come to a picture of a horse. As I look at the picture, I can sense the Holy Spirit, knowing that this is a gift from the Lord. This young man has named the picture "The Horse." As I look at the picture I notice a scripture in the right-hand corner:

Proverbs 21:31 (ESV)
The horse is made ready for the day of battle, but the
victory belongs to the Lord.

I actually wanted to cry because I knew what God was saying. He was saying, "Yes, I am making you ready, I am your healer, I am your restorer, I am your Father who loves you."

With one scripture the Lord brought complete clarity to what He is teaching me using this TV show and these horses. The horse is being made ready and we are each that horse. The horse, it reflects and feels everything we feel, just as our Savior Jesus does.

This horse represents the restoration and healing God wants to provide in our lives, but the Lord also showed me in my dream at the beginning of this book that there is a bear – an invisible spiritual force working against this process. The scriptures say that we do not war against flesh and blood but against principalities, powers and wickedness in heavenly places. (Ephesians 6:12) We are in a battle. You may ask what is the battle about? It is for the souls of the people, but ultimately it is about satan blocking our restoration and taking away our purpose and our voice for the Kingdom of God.

"The Horse" picture now hangs in my office and is a daily reminder not only of how much God cares and loves us but also that He is preparing us. It also reminds me that Jesus has already won this battle! He is the one who rides the white horse, and we who believe will be riding right behind Him.

Let the Lord prepare you. Let Him heal you.

Revelation 19:11 (NIV)
"I saw heaven standing open and there before me
was a white horse, whose rider is called
Faithful and True."
Rise up. Be prepared. Our restorer The King is coming.

Dear Lord,

You are the one who restores all things new. We thank You that we are being made ready. Lord, help us to be ready. Let us not slumber nor sleep, for this is a time to rise up and be prepared. Help us to have a supernatural ability to hear the Holy Spirit, for we know that the Kingdom of Heaven is close and our Redeemer is drawing near.

In Jesus' name. Amen.

Jeremiah 46:3-4 (NIV)
"Prepare your shields, both large and small, and march
out for battle! Harness the horses, mount the steeds! Take
your positions with helmets on! Polish your spears, put on
your armor!"

Matthew 24:42-43 (NASB)
"Therefore be on the alert, for you do not know which day your Lord is coming. But be sure of this, that if the head of the house had known at what time of the night the thief was coming, he would have been on the alert and would not have allowed his house to be broken into."

IN CLOSING

In my first book *Redeemed*, God showed how He had snatched me and others out of the hand of our enemy. He never quits looking for us. He never quits trying to send us messages of love. We cannot even fathom how much God loves each of us. If you try to compare His love, it would be like loving your own children times a billion, and remember that He gave us our children so He loves them more than we do.

In this book, God is talking to us about restoration, getting prepared, rising up from your ashes, standing firm in your faith, holding the ground God has given you, being bold for Christ. In order to do these things we have to be made ready, healed and whole, because if we are not, our enemy will use it against us.

What I want to say is: don't ever forget who you are in Christ. If you want to know the truth, listen to Jesus because His love is real, unwavering, unchanging, and never-ending. His love covers a multitude of sins and will set you free! Love is not a feeling, it is a decision, and the day Jesus gave up His life for you and me, He made a decision to love us. You and I have been bought by the good Master! Can you even imagine as Heaven watched from above while Jesus was on that cross? He died, went down into hell, and took back the keys! (Revelation 1:18 KJV) And then on the 3rd day rose from the dead! Heaven had been waiting for Jesus to come back home! Heaven now awaits us as the table is being prepared! The Groom is coming for His bride, so get ready. Be like the wise brides and be prepared. (Matthew 25:1-13)

If you would like to share your own testimony or you have questions, I would love to hear from you!

my email is:

savedbyjesus2018@gmail.com

PRAYER OF SALVATION

Pray this prayer out loud:

Heavenly Father, I come to You in the name of Jesus and by the Blood of Christ,.

I repent of my sins against You and ask You to come into my heart, mind, body, soul and spirit, and be my Lord and Savior. I believe You died for my sins and rose on the third day and You are now seated at the right hand of the Father. I ask You to fill me with Your Holy Spirit, and help me on this journey we are starting right now.

Thank You for not giving up on me and for saving me.

In Jesus' name. Amen

If you have given your life to Jesus, I would love to hear from you:

savedbyjesus2018@gmail.com

43045917R00048

Made in the USA
Lexington, KY
23 June 2019